INTO THIS WORLD

ALSO BY
MICHAEL MILLER

The Joyful Dark
The Singing Inside
Darkening the Grass

INTO THIS WORLD

POEMS BY
MICHAEL MILLER

PINYON PUBLISHING
Montrose, Colorado

Cover photograph by Gary L. Entsminger

Book and Cover Design by Susan E. Elliott

Photograph of Michael Miller by Mary Moran

First Edition: April 2013

Pinyon Publishing
23847 V66 Trail, Montrose, CO 81403
www.pinyon-publishing.com

Library of Congress Control Number: 2013934941
ISBN: 978-1-936671-14-4

Acknowledgments

Some of these poems, in slightly different versions, have appeared in *Commonweal, North American Review, Pinyon Review, Raritan, Rattle, Sow's Ear Poetry Review, The Yale Review*, and *Leafing Out*, a chapbook published by Finishing Line Press.

For Mary

No love without sympathy
—Emerson

CONTENTS

I

II

III

IV

The Song of the Body   49

V

I

CRACKS

My black coffee is cooling down,
Early light falls through the window
Where I sit beside the spider
Crawling out of cracks in the house.
I let it live. I turn from
Deliberate death in the newspaper
To draw the sweet life out of an orange
Before I walk down Heatherstone Road.
I stand beneath a cardinal singing
On the telephone wire. Black mask,
Black news. I envy this red crested bird
Who knows nothing of Afghanistan,
Of the fifteen-year-old girl
With half her face a map of scars
From the acid thrown as she walked to school.
She has refused to cover the scars.
She is more determined to become
The woman she has been told she cannot be.

GUARDIANS

The ghosts of soldiers killed in Iraq
Are going to Afghanistan, weary of Mosul,
Of Ramadi, of the complaining marketers
Who can no longer sell grease guns, RPGs.
The ghosts have forgotten which of
These weapons cut short their lives.
Now another war is swelling like a dead
Water buffalo floating in the Euphrates;
There are more troops arriving in Kabul,
More young men, more young women.
Each ghost knows he cannot protect them all.

TRUST

He has been conditioned to act
Without a moment's hesitation.
It might be harder if he saw
Their faces, if he were close enough
To look into their eyes—
But it makes no difference to the bullet.
He has held each one between his
Forefinger and thumb, caressing it
As if it were a woman's nipple.
In Afghanistan, far from any woman
That he drew into his tattooed arms,
He names his bullets Sue Ellen, Mary,
Loretta, trusting them implicitly,
Keeping them immaculate.

PRIVATE BAYLESS

Before the dark shoulders of mountains,
Setting forth on a night mission
With the wind's breath
Blowing across his face, pricking him
With invisible needles of sand,
He smells death in the air.
"The Taliban, the Taliban," a voice
Gnaws at his mind, and he prays
To leave Afghanistan alive, intact.
Should a bullet sever his spinal cord,
He will make love to his wife
With his eyes, blinking signals
For the acts he cannot perform.

BURIED

In Helmand Province, in farming villages,
They buried their rifles in hay,
Then went into the fields with the cows,
Waiting to return and rule.
Everyone knew the Taliban,
Everyone except his platoon.

HM1 KINNEY

His blood remembers blood,
The musky, metallic smell,
How it soaked dressing
After dressing, how he stuffed
Kerlix into the mouths of wounds.

The femoral artery pumped blood
He couldn't stop,
The vitals plummeted,
The dried blood darkened
Beneath his fingernails.

"Corpsman up, corpsman up!"
He hears them shout
At the dead end of a dream
And wakes up running toward
A man he has to save.

PRIVATE WHEELER

Adrift in a morphine haze,
He closes his eyes
And strips down his rifle,
Spreading the parts on his poncho,
Wiping the bolt,
Oiling the lands and grooves
Inside the barrel,
Moving his hands with
Unbearable tenderness,
Forgetting they are gone.

CORPORAL BEDFORD

He is coughing up ashes,
Black ashes from the burnt dead
Left in the charred truck
Abandoned on the roadside,
The dead who dance in his dream,
A circle around him,
Their hands linked in a chain.

He can never escape,
Never return to the man
He was before the war,
The man who found joy
In the wriggling trout
He raised from the stream
Sparkling like diamonds.

LANCE CORPORAL WEBSTER

Call him the half-limbed man,
Though you would never know it
With his shirt and trousers covering
His artificial arms and legs.
While he undresses, a titanium man
Will greet your pitying eyes.
He stops and starts his life
Like the microprocessors
Inside his prosthetic limbs.
He was an ordinary man,
An enlisted man,
Before his one wrong step
Into that roadside bomb.

SERGEANT GOMEZ

He stares at his uniform
Spread on his bed like a corpse,
His Marine Corps Dress Blues,
And with his mother's scissors
Cuts the royal blue trousers
With a red stripe running down
Each leg and then the dark
Blue jacket, beginning with
The sleeves and cutting
Through the red and yellow
Sergeant chevrons. He saves
The rows of ribbons for last,
The Purple Heart, Bronze Star,
Then cuts cleanly, precisely,
And holds them like pieces
Of a broken rainbow,
Remembering that father carrying
His daughter draped over his arms
With bullet holes stitched across
Her white dress
And blood like shiny buttons.

CORPORAL SAYERS

He accepts each day as if it were
A registered letter:
The sun, the storm, the hail
Beating against the roof with the sound
Of machine-gun bullets he once fired.
There was nothing he could do about the war,
The designed killing,
The accidental killing,
The murder that few would call murder.
He used no sniper's scope,
He never saw the faces of the men he killed.
The war is over,
The dead will not run across a ridgeline,
And he has returned,
Refusing to kill a spider.

II

OLD FRIENDS

Crossing the field, I enter the woods
To be with the reliable hemlock,
The pin oak, the white pine;
I say their names as if they were
Old friends. Once I climbed branches
To make a nest for my dreams,
To persuade the wind to favor me
With its blessing, but now I can only
Gaze upward, standing beside roots
Like gnarled fingers of an ancient hand.

DUSK

I comb carefully my remaining hair;
All my losses have been gradual.
No loved one has been ripped from my life
Like a flowering branch broken off.
I cling to cherished possessions;
My son's youthful drawings,
The letters from friends yellowing
Like the long grass of late September
On the meadow where I walk at dusk,
Knowing the darkness will arrive
With a part of me welcoming it.

BURIED LOVE

I

"Joanna died," my friend whispered
That first day of school,
"Over the summer, leukemia."
And my voice fell into a place
Inside my fourteen-year-old being,
Never to utter her name again.
In my seventieth winter
I still carry that buried love.

II

I have no photographs of Joanna—
What I remember are
Her cheekbones, smooth planes
I wanted to stroke, her green eyes
Gazing into the distance
Without a question,
Her fourteen summers ripped
Like a blossom from a branch.

III

At twenty-one, beautiful,
Vibrant, she appeared in my dream,
Crossing a meadow
Where the burst milkweed pods
Hung like empty shells.
Dark dark her unjust death,
White cells devouring the red.

IV

She has been hibernating
Through the decades and will soon
Appear, entering the kitchen where
I sit with black coffee, the newspaper.
She will bring me nothing
Of the horrors, the deaths,
The immensity of suffering,
Only her innocence asking,
"What happened?"

HARD

I bite into the rye crust of toast,
Hearing it crunch, relishing the hardness.
I have always been drawn to the hard:
The stubbled face of Pine Cobble Mountain,
The rock garden I tended through the years.
My body was hard once, but now
My pectorals remind me of breasts,
Your breasts that press against my own.
It was always love I sought,
Never empty sex, only the hard love,
The love that would last.

NO MATTER OUR AGE

I remember stroking your breast
That first time;
The moment bore into my heart
Then hidden from you
But not from the life I dreamt of.
More than your body
I wanted the love
Which flickered in your eyes.
So our unwritten history began
Which I value each morning,
Waking to its freshness
No matter our age
Or the architecture
Crumbling around us.

HANDS

The iridescent bird inside you
Had flown out to escape the hands
Refusing to tuck you in that night.
Years later it returned,
A tattoo upon your left shoulder.

I touched your hair as I once
Touched the keys playing Chopin,
Careful not to disturb
The delicacy of each note.
My fingers moved gently upon you,
A lover's fingers not your father's.

Turning from the long scars,
The parallel lines upon your thighs
That you were driven to inflict
With his razor blade,
I only saw the smooth,
Untouched skin between them.

Together, we buried the past.
After the funeral, we walked
Toward spring, over the perennials
Waiting to emerge
Beneath that lid of earth.

MORNING WALK

As sunlight leans over the tops of pines
And brightens the faces of old houses,
We pass the same gardens
Blooming along our quiet street.
We choose different flowers to look at,
We see different birds,
But we begin each day without each other,
Not wanting any eyes other than our own.
Later, there are two versions
Of the same story to tell;
The yellow-throated warbler
Or the purple finch, the leaning lily
Or the salmon rose.

ROSE

A drift of beauty
Will fall with each petal
As permanence eludes us.
All we can experience is now:
The summer breeze
Blowing through lace,
Our bodies sending messages
As we lie naked,
The rose beside our bed,
Its leaning stem a bend
In the late afternoon.

MEETING

Upon meeting, we leaned toward
Each other on that winter's day
When the cold ignited something hidden,
Something waiting to burn within us.
Years passed. Time, an unseen sheath,
Held us silently together,
Aging us without our consent.

UNFADED

My fingers and tongue still find
Their place upon your lounging breasts,
Between your matrimonial thighs—
My desire for you has not faded.
A woman half your age smiled at me
But it was your face, your shoulders I saw
Drawing me towards you once again.

WINTER'S END

Imagine, now, the abundance of blossoms
When the leftover rags of snow melt
Around the nine magnolia trees circling
Cleopatra's Needle in Central Park;
Imagine the surrounding pink-and-white beauty
When winter's end is behind us
And we, without a word, stand gratefully
Together, needing nothing more to tell us
That beauty can be achieved, that praise
Will be more welcome than condemnation.
Yesterday two robins rose from a mat
Of yellowed grass in parallel lines,
Beaks touching amid a flutter of wings.
We are too old to mate, my love,
But we are still part of the dance.

III

ANOTHER LANGUAGE

Far from childhood's brutal muting
Fatherhood brought another language
I could speak without the slightest hesitation.
I filled the hollowness my father left,
I became the one who stayed.

DRUM

It was the turtle I remember
Basking on the oil drum jutting from
The shallows of the pond
As my son stepped forward slowly,
Not trying to catch him
With his wrinkled neck
Craning into the breeze
But to look closer,
His wide-eyed stare fastened to
One small turtle,
The way I moved closer to look upon
His small body bent over the table
As he painted blue turtles
Flying away from the drum.

GOLDFINCH

O yellow breast and black wings,
Fly from this ten-foot sunflower
And let your streak of beauty
Brighten the new day,
Declare yourself in full flight
Letting instinct carry you.
O yellowest of goldfinches
Winged with dark but born of light,
Brighten my way,
Comrade of enduring light.

CAGED

The caged polar bear presses against
The steel bars as if to wear them away
But only succeeds in leaving
An indentation like a white part
On his triangular head.
His urgent quest continues along
The circumference of his cage
Past unruly children, distracted parents.
This graceful nomad will never bound
Through an Arctic dawn, never mate,
Never smash his head into ice
To drag a seal between the cracks.
He will die hungering for what
The memories in his blood demand.

HUNGER

Black feathered bodies huddle,
Bobbing heads yank out the guts
Of a headless deer left in the woods,
Feasting beneath pines
That glisten with needles of light.

I watch and learn nothing;
Nothing more about the hunter
Who wanted another head for his wall,
Nothing more about the deer
That leapt into his eyes,
Nothing more about the hungering crows.

Yet there remains a constant hunger
For the goodness, unaffected,
That can gradually change us, fill us,
And move quietly into this world.

TALONS

Beating upon the hawk's heavy wings
The rain arrives like an assailant,
Sweeping down the mountain,
Soaking the field, matting my hair.
Even in a summer storm the hawk
Must eat; it plummets, it seizes
A trembling rabbit between its trap
Of talons, ripping through fur.
Neither hawk nor rabbit, my blood
Exults while my brain say, "Go home."

EACH NIGHT

In the pale glow of the porch light
I see him at eleven o'clock each night,
Walking slowly across the backyard,
His pointed head navigating the way,
His tail like a long wire
Connected to the dark.
On his path of desire this possum
Moves toward what he may never find.
In his routine he serves some purpose—
To attain what he needs
At the long end of the night.

BURROWING

On this April morning
When I approach the forsythia
Like a mound of waiting gold
Or the quince like a thousand
Pink bells that cannot ring,
I burrow into the silence
Like the black-and-yellow bumble bee
That lands in a quince blossom,
Its six legs as thin as eyelashes
Moving slowly until it finds
A world beyond itself.

THE INVISIBLE LIFE

My very old dog continually licks
The floor for crumbs that are
Not there, the instinct to live
Drives his bent body from stove
To sink to table. He is trying to lick
The invisible life from the floor
As he wobbles from room to room
Before his crooked legs give out.
I lift him so he can continue,
Oblivious, as the life seeps out
Of his bewildered body
That I stroke every night
And the first thing each morning.

LETTING GO

Not by choice am I alone in these woods
Where my son accompanied me years ago,
But he is in a thronging city
While I, passing berries like drops of fire,
Pause by the pond where the frogs
Still float like bloated kings
In their green courtyards of algae.

Somewhere in his travels
My son may remember how we waded into water
And tried to catch the frogs
That squirmed between our fingers.
Those frogs, those speckled
Slippery bodies that once slid through
Our hands, were never meant for us to keep.

FOREVER

What I began, he continued,
And each bedtime story
Drew us together
In the soft lamplight

Until we no longer seemed
A father, a son,
But creators of a kingdom
Ruled by a dancing dragon

Or a universe where we slid down
The smooth side of Mars
Into a constellation
We named Forever.

LADYBUGS

Ladybugs dapple the screen;
Their tiny feet fit perfectly
Into the network of wire.
I wait for the first to move
Through the hole and bring
Autumn's blaze into the room.
What momentum carries them forward,
Their smallness no less significant
Than the eagle's wingspan or the elephant
Gracing the plains with its bulk.

THE PORCH LIGHT

My neighbor's porch light
Burns through the night,
It brightens the locked screen door,
The heavy wooden one.
She wants to keep
The men of violence away,
The unknown man who raped her
Years ago, in that distant city.
Now she lives with dogs around her,
With pines and grass.
But he is still out there,
Stalking in a different guise,
His blank emotionless face,
His granite eyes, looking for
An entrance, an opening,
An unlocked window.
He has not changed,
He is still driven to get in.

PIT BULL

Not a face locked in malevolence,
Not a compact machine of menace,
My neighbor's pit bull
With a slow, bow-legged gait
Sniffs the heat-stricken grass
And lifts his head to gaze at me.
I bend to stroke him,
Running my hand along his smooth back,
Every preconception I held vanishing.

AUGURY

I watch a great blue heron
Fly over the cornfield, balancing
The sky upon its wide wings,
Its soundless flight delivering
A message to be deciphered.
I want to glide through each day
With such grace,
With no conscious struggle
For the difficult.
But man is no bird—
He must labor for the clear thought,
The graceful line, the right words
In the right place
For the blank, white page.

SAFE HOUSE

A terrified deer bounds across
The meadow, outdistancing a coyote
Chasing it into the woods.
I feel death's cold breath
On the bristling beard of the wind,
Then hurry up the tree-shadowed road,
Returning to the safe house
To ease my body into bed,
Pressing firmly against you.

IV

THE SONG OF THE BODY

I

When they dwell in the kingdom of appetite
Where the lords of lust
And the queens of desire rule,
Where fantasy dances in a cobbled courtyard,
They celebrate the song of the body,
Of ageless, silent harmonies.

II

Everything seems to fall away:
The sunlight slanting through the window,
The ceiling fan like oars stroking
Midsummer air until nothing exists
Except her; the width of her shoulders
Like a white egret's wings descending,
Her face becoming nothing but eyes.

III

He tries to gaze beyond her body,
Past the beauty of shoulders,
Of breasts, of thighs articulate
With strength. It is not this
That matters, not the symmetry,
Not the uniqueness of one breast
Larger than the other; it is
The foreignness inside her,
The part unknown to him.

IV

They surrender to their passion
As words and definitions fall away
Like old inheritances; their fingers,
Lips, and tongues touching anew.
Now they never say each other's name,
Now they never whisper, "I love you,"
Now they forget everything:
The achievements, the possessions,
The orderly house they have built,
All vanishing, all immersed
In the pure joy.

V

He moves inside her as she pulses
With his rhythm, and it is their bodies' music,
The harmonies of flesh that captivate,
Then bring them to fulfillment
Until he slips away, spent,
The song gone out of him.

VI

Now their bodies fit the journey,
Moving slower but not ungracefully.
The distance, the places recede—
The Tuileries at dawn, the wet leaves
Like yellow handprints upon the pathways,
And their top room on the rue Royale
Overlooking the jumble of rooftops.
Paris remains inside them, unchanged.

VII

How effortlessly they have always
Come together, but now, with his penis
Sleepwalking through their lovemaking,
He is joined to her by the tenderness
That her smile bestows, that her hands
Unfold, and this is nearly enough.

VIII

He could take the small blue pill
Before they make love, assuring that
He would keep the remembered firmness,
But he chooses to drift toward
The invisible borders of sleep,
Imagining this is a silent forecast
Of the long sleep to come.

IX

He has embraced her body's changes,
The widening hips after the birth,
The firm breasts that have become pendulous.
She rests her head upon his cushion
Of stomach, not the drum-skin
She once playfully punched.
Love has moved beyond their bodies,
Beyond what they see, what they touch.

X

Their blue sheets are the color
Of the irises blooming in their garden,
Bordering the two-foot stone wall;
They planted the irises,
They built the wall,
Their hands know earth, stone,
And now they continue to seek
The undiscovered regions
Of each other's body,
The new concealed within the old.

XI

They rise and leave the sheets,
The rippled shallows of their loving
And await the dark's arrival;
Even death has no recourse
Except to unwind itself
Like the thread from a spool
On an ageless tailor's shelf.
They have no loose ends to follow
Back to the past, only the future
With its woven surprises.

XII

Their bodies' youthful equilibrium
Once seemed to keep death away,
Beyond the kissing of the smooth flesh,
The touching of the tenderest unseen.
But death has always been inside of them,
An invisible rider nothing can throw off.

XIII

He glimpses his end
In moments of impenetrable loneliness,
In the silence beyond sleep.
Aware of his fear, she offers
Her body to soothe him,
Feeling a completion
When her breast is between
His hands, her nipple in his mouth,
His head burrowing into
A room in her heart.

V

THE VAULT

At dawn he sits at the kitchen table,
Brushing the crumbs away, a white-haired man
Unlocking the vault of his past.
He writes in his forgiving diary,
Releasing the ghosts haunting his dreams,
Learning love has outdistanced anger.
His hand moves slowly, the blood-sown ink
Creating his mother's image,
The blur of his father,
His comrades exploding on Guadalcanal.
He is discovering that each word leads him
Into feelings he had chosen not to confront,
Burying them with his mistakes,
Covering over their deaths.

AT THE EMERALD PUB

Inconspicuous in a shadowed corner,
His eyes closed for a moment
And the unwanted thoughts return—
The waves of killing have changed
But death remains the same,
The tide of blood continuing,
Its steady flow still in his dreams,
Reddening the sand of each island.
He remembers the lives deprived
Of their future, the letters
He was asked to mail, "In case,"
And with each whiskey and cigarette
Another comrade appears, his face
Still innocent across the table.

OKINAWA

The machinery of war standing in
The rice paddies never enters his dreams,
Nor do the typhoons bent on catastrophe
Or the binjo ditches outside each house.
But she is always with him; Sumiko,
After the raucous bar closed,
Eating with him in the quiet restaurant
In Terragawa, cutting her hamburger in half
With the precision of a surgeon.
"My mother is hungry," she whispered,
Wrapping it neatly in a napkin.
This is what he kept from that bloody island,
The hunger filling Sumiko with compassion
That startled him from every excess.

PIECES

He remembers the smoothness of each piece,
Of each particular shape
Always cold to his touch,
The slide and click of the bolt,
The long length of barrel,
The muzzle a hole into the dark.
Placing each piece on his blanket
He cleaned them lovingly
With toothbrush, oil, and rag,
Saving the small, curved trigger for last,
Then assembled the immaculate rifle,
His beautiful weapon ready for killing.
What did his eighteen years know about war
On the drill fields of Parris Island,
About dangling intestines,
An artery pumping blood like a fountain?

IN THE ALBUM

The loneliness of the young Marines
Remains hidden; he is the sergeant
In that photograph, his longing pressed
Into the creases of his Dress Blues.
It was not about glory, country;
What bound them, held them was the way,
Together, they held their rifles,
Drawing them close to their chests at port arms.
Now his hair is white, his body bent.
He closes his album, returns it to the past,
And wonders which of them is dead.

BEARING

Reminding him of bullets
He once slid into the rifle's
Immaculate chamber,
The smooth magnolia buds
Blossom; they do not kill.
When winds lash the branches
And snow covers their shivering surface,
They keep their bearing.
All winter he looks at them,
Removing a glove to touch.
Soon the branches will be
Hidden by a cloud of blossoms,
Their pink-and-white petals
Exploding into spring.

BURNING

A man ignited from within
Brightens the night,
Striding alone through a meadow,
Singeing the grass,
Alarming the milkweed.

He is beyond the reach of rain
And wants help from no one.
This fire has blazed
In his dark time, in his need,
Keeping him alive.

RECOLLECTION

As quietly as the child
Counting on his fingers
He recalls the ones he loved,
Their gentle harmonies
That kept them close,
Their deaths a sigh of mortality.
Some he never said goodbye to,
Others he held as if they could resist
The piracy of the dark.

FIVE A.M.

Through the network of naked branches
He gazes at the full moon, opening his hand,
Imagining the moon is resting in his palm,
Its lovely wholeness in contrast to his
Life's incompleteness, his life without
His son, now grown, and gone, leaving only
A triangle broken. "Love her," the moon whispers,
"Love your wife." "I do," he says, drawing back
His hand. "Love her more," the moon warns him—
He waits for the scrim of cloud to cover it
Like a cataract, but the moon shines on.

RUE CAMBON

He remembered her arm extending only to the elbow,
As smooth as the round handle
Of his grandfather's ivory cane.
And he loved her from the stump inward:
How she sauntered under the chestnut blossoms
When he first saw her;
How her lips filled the room on the rue Cambon.
She brought goodness into his life
To carry with him through the years.

THE DANCING

When the shades of his eyes closed
The dancing began, his mother large in his arms,
Her folds of flesh hanging beneath her shoulders,
Then his wife, her lithe body swaying
Like the tasseled willow.
It was the dancing that pushed away the world,
That brushed him with a fragrance,
A wisp of flowing hair.

QUINCE

From a distance the quince blossoms
Blur in the brightening day;
He has forgotten his glasses again,
Now resting in his robe's frayed pocket.
When he moves closer, breaking off
A branch for his wife,
He is oblivious to the numerous bees
Zigzagging around the dense bush
Like yellow-vested guardians.
He only sees the dark pink blossoms,
Imagining them in her hand.

THE WEEDS

The weeds advance to strangle
The dahlias, cleomes, foxgloves,
And run like thieves
Across their sumptuous garden.
But on their hands and knees
They probe with fingers seeking out
These bold insurgents
Until they grip and yank one out,
Keeping what they plant alive,
Undeterred by how soon
The others will arrive.

FRAYED

Walking through the dark house
Wearing only a frayed pajama top
And gripping his penis, he murmurs,
"What is this, what is this?"
She hears his voice as in a dream,
And with sorrow as deep as her love
Leads him back to bed.
At breakfast he tells her
His brain is diseased but his mind is good.
He talks about their garden,
Then passes her the blueberries
Which burst with fresh sweetness.

THE NET

If she sits beside the hospital bed,
If she takes his hand and keeps on talking
She might be able to keep him alive,
Letting the words manufacture a life,
Letting them bring him a world that will not
Tremble as his emaciated body trembles
With each short, arduous breath.
She begins by telling him how
The purple finches fly from the sycamore
To the telephone wire, how every day
Arrives with something new,
Something different, and if she looks
Carefully enough she will see it,
She will remember and return tomorrow
And tell him because she wants him to live!
She will summon every word she knows
And give them gently to him, spreading them
Like a net that captures a world.

CPSIA information can be obtained at www.ICGtesting.com
Printed in the USA
LVOW131911010413

327093LV00001B/27/P